30 DAYS IN THE LIFE OF A MAD TEACHER

30 DAYS IN THE LIFE OF A MAD TEACHER

BREN BERRY

Cover Art by: Raynald Kudemus

Copyright © 2024 **Bren Berry Publishing**

All rights reserved. No part of this publication may be reproduced, distributed, or transmitted in any form or by any means, including photocopying, recording, or other electronic or mechanical methods, without the prior written permission of the publisher, except in the case of brief quotations embodied in critical reviews and certain other noncommercial uses permitted by copyright law. For permission requests, write to the publisher, addressed "Attention: Book Rights and Permission," at the address below.

Published in the United States of America

ISBN 978-1-960159-34-2 (SC)
ISBN 978-1-962730-73-0 (HC)

Bren Berry Publishing
222 West 6th Street
Suite 400, San Pedro, CA, 90731
www.stellarliterary.com

Ordering Information and Rights Permission:
Quantity sales. Special discounts might be available on quantity purchases by corporations, associations, and others. For details, contact the publisher at the address above.

For Book Rights Adaptation and other Rights Permission. Call us at toll-free 1-888-945-8513 or send us an email at admin@stellarliterary.com.

Contents

Introduction v
   Monday Morning 1
   Monday Morning 5
   The Next Day 9
   Anymore Questions? 11
   Before We Leave 15
   The Next Morning 18
   Monday Morning 20
   Test Day 23
   The Next Day 24
   The End of the Week 26
   The Next Morning 29
   Friday Morning 30

Introduction

Let me explain how I happened to get this job. After graduating from college and taking off to rest for a year, it was kindly suggested by my parents that I get a job. In fact, a friend of my father came by and told us that the local school district was hiring, and they desperately needed teachers; and as long as I could count without using my fingers and toes, I had a good shot at the job.

It sounded good to me. I mean how difficult could it be to be locked in a room with twenty- five little kids; after all, I was so much bigger than they were. What about the summers off and all those holidays. I thought, what a great job. Looking back in retrospect, it was the only job that you needed summer, winter, spring, and fall off. And despite that, some of the teachers don't make it back for the new school year—they needed more time!

I was late to work this morning; well actually, I'm late most mornings. I'll bet you are wondering, how I keep my job? That's simple, no one else wants it, and if you keep reading, you'll understand why.

If you think this is going to be a traditional diary or a blow-by-blow description of daily events, you are sadly mistaken. I don't have time for that. I will, however, tell you where we are in the stream of time. You will just have to accept my word that these events transpired approximately when I stated; however, they may not be in strict chronological order due to the fact that I seemed to have lost my focus in life.

I had hoped for a better class this year, or at least one that was as funny as last year's class.

Of course, who could forget Denny the Dentist? Now Denny wasn't fit to practice. I based that assumption on the fact that he was only ten years old and unlicensed. Do you know that the parents actually thought he was a real dentist and they went looking for him? The only reason he got busted was that the janitor found his receipt book and two baby teeth behind the cafeteria! Had he not gotten caught, he probably would have moved on to oral surgery. You'd think that all of us would have been wiser, but we attributed the inordinate number of toothless children to their over consumption of candy.

Then there was Brittany stalking Ryan. I remember it got so bad until I asked the principal for a restraining order. Of course, he told me that children can't get restraining orders. I said "yeah," but they don't have to know that. "Why don't we issue a fake restraining order stating that they had to stay at least twenty feet from each other?"

He agreed, it worked, at lease for a while.

Since both of them were mathematically impaired, they weren't quite sure where twenty feet was, so they thought it would be a good idea to meet up in the cafeteria each morning with tape measure in hand and measured off twenty feet. Well, as mentioned, it worked a while. Then we began to notice that each morning, while eating breakfast in the cafeteria, they seemed to get closer and closer each day until finally, Brittany ended up in Ryan's lap. It was only then that we realized that they had serious problems with spatial relationships. Despite the fact that this situation has not been resolved, we still are going to move on.

Monday Morning

As I was preparing for the new school year, in walks Principal Daniels. "Good morning, Ms. Berry. I have a really big favor to ask of you. As you know, we have a much larger enrollment than we anticipated. Therefore, we have a teacher shortage, so I need you to move to the next campus over and take over the sixth grade, but for only thirty days. I promise I'll have a new teacher by then."

"Well, what happened to their teacher?" I asked.

"As you know, they locked her in the closet the last day of school. And at the last minute, she decided that she was going to retire."

"Well, the sixth grade started yesterday, what happened to the substitute?"

"She didn't make it out of her car."

"Okay, okay, but thirty days only. Why do you think I can handle them?" "Well for one thing, you can be a bit scary," said the principal smiling.

"Well, that's true," I sheepishly agreed.

"Besides, Ms. Berry, your reputation precedes you and many of the kids in this class were in your first kindergarten class," said Mr. Daniels.

"Okay, I'll give it a shot" I said.

"I'd choose my words more wisely," mumbled Mr. Daniels.

Okay, okay what do I do? I need a game plan. It has been my experience that they are usually good the first few days of school, and then their true personalities begin to emerge. The clowns came out first immediately followed by the drama queens.

I have to get them before they get me. In order to do that, I know that I will have to reveal something personal about them, but not too personal, after all I don't want to get into trouble.

Huh, it might work and it's worth a try. Oh, I hear some of them coming.

"Hello class, please come in and find your name tags. Now I know that you are no longer in kindergarten, but sometimes, adults wear name tags at seminars and conventions and it's just for a few days until I get to know you. Now, I realize that you don't know me," I said.

"We know you," said Rizzo. "Me, Rollo, Leo, Richie, and Missy were in your first kindergarten class"

"Oh, I do remember some of you. Well, it is so nice to see that you have survived and made it all the way to the sixth grade."

"Ms. Berry?"

"Yes, Leo?"

"Do you remember you tried to spank me when I was five and weighed sixty pounds? I'm now twelve and weigh 160 pounds. I don't think you'll be trying to spank me today," said Leo.

"I see your point," I said.

"Because of you I hate school. I hate reading, writing, math, science, history, and geography. I also hate books, pencils, paper ink, erasers, and pens," yelled Leo.

I can't let him get away with that, it will undermine my authority. I'll lose control. Let me think of something that will put me back in control.

"Leo, I remember you well. Are you still afraid of clowns?"

"No, teacher," said Leo. "I got over that fear years ago."

"Good because the circus is coming to town and I'll make sure you get tickets." Leo now turns red in the face. The class then started smiling. Good, now I have the class back under my control.

"Teacher!"

"Yes, Richie"

"I hate school too because of you."

"Richie, are you still afraid of twins?"

"No, teacher" replied Richie, "after I found out that it wasn't the same person in two places."

"What clued you in?" I asked.

"Well, it was the Jensen twins. I realized one was a girl and the other one was a boy."

"Richie, you're still as sharp as a marble," I quipped. "Boys and girls, I'm going to let you go a little early today, so that you can start making preparations for the big dance this weekend, is everyone going?" I see a hand in the back. "Yes, Rizzo," I said.

"Teacher, I have a tux, a limo, and a corsage. I have everything but a date." "Rizzo, what happened? When you were in kindergarten, you were so popular."

"Well, you know I had poison ivy over the summer and it left me with a rash, but the girls don't believe me, so they run when they see me."

"I'm sorry to hear that," I said. "Is there anything I can do to help?"

"Yeah, you can get me a date?"

"How?" I asked.

"Ms. Berry, can you hook me up with Matchbox.com?"

"Well, I don't think they cater to pre-teens, and besides it takes time to check people out. Well," I said, "I'll try to find you a date. Girls, is there anyone who wants to go, but does not have a date? Missy, do I see your hand up? Well, the bell is about to ring, so why don't you and Rizzo meet after class?"

"Okay, Missy," said Rizzo, "do you want to go to the dance with me?"

"Yeah, I'll go," said Missy.

"Will you be wearing a mask?" asked Rizzo.

"No, stupid it's not a masquerade party," shouted Missy. "So why don't you just go with your cousin, you know the one that needs to shave?" Missy now walks off.

"Class, take pictures, and we will talk about the dance on Monday."

Monday Morning

"Class, how was the dance?" I asked.

"Great," shouted Rizzo.

"How was your cousin?" asked Missy.

"At least I had a date," said Rizzo.

"I had a date too," replied Missy.

"You were there? How come no one saw you?"

"I had on a white Cinderella dress and golden stilettos" said Missy.

"That was you? Dang you looked good!" said Rizzo.

"Why didn't you get up and dance?" asked Missy.

"I got benched," said Rizzo.

"How do you get benched at a dance?" asked Missy.

"The teachers didn't like my moves and besides, I didn't like the music," said Rizzo.

"But weren't you in charge of the music?" asked Missy

The bell rings and Rizzo runs down the hall without answering.

After recess he returns to the room.

"Class, don't forget the parent—teacher's meeting in two weeks, and I want to see everyone's parents, said Ms. Berry."

"Richie, are your parents coming?" asked Rizzo.

"Yeah, are yours coming?" asked Richie.

"No, my parents are deceased."

"Does that mean they're not coming?" asked Richie.

"It means that they are dead."

"Oh, I'm sorry. I'll send you a card."

"Okay, class, settle down."

"Okay, class, to get better acquainted with you, especially those of you I don't know, I want you to stand up and tell me a little about yourselves.

"Okay young man at the back in the yellow shirt."

"Hi, my name is Max, and I'm twelve years old, and I want to be an attorney when I grow up and if that don't work out, I want to be a lawyer," said Max.

"Max," yelled Melvin, "go get a dictionary."

Max comes back with an encyclopedia. Melvin yells, "Man that ain't a dictionary. When you open a dictionary, it says Mary Ann Webster."

"I believe that's Merriam Webster" I said.

"Teacher, did she change her name?" asked Melvin.

"No, I don't think so!" I said.

"Okay, class. Let's move on," I said. "Who's next? The young man in blue."

"Hello, my name is Dexter and I want to be a veterinarian or either a kid doctor," said Dexter.

"What noble professions," I said. "So why do you want to be a veterinarian?"

"So I can help the veterans when they came back from wars," replied Dexter.

"Oh, I don't think you understand what a veterinarian is. He's an animal doctor," I said.

"Animal doctor!" shouts Dexter, "Oh, I'm afraid of animals, maybe I'll become a kid doctor," said Dexter.

"You mean a pediatrician," I said.

"Yeah, whatever," replied Dexter. "If I can become a doctor while I'm a kid that will be great," said Dexter.

"No, I don't think you understand," I said. "A pediatrician is an adult doctor who works on kids."

"Oh, I hate kids," shouted Dexter.

"Then you can't be a pediatrician!" I said.

"They don't have to know I don't like them."

"They'll know," I said, tugging at my hair. "Does anyone have an aspirin?"

"No," said Rizzo, "this is a drug free school."

"Okay, I'll take one more student today" I said.

"Next, the boy with the green hair."

"My name is Filo Quincy Mardon, and I want to play for the Lakers."

"Filo, I'm assuming that you are about twelve years old and you look like you are about 4'11", you need a backup plan."

"Oh, okay, I want to play for the Clippers," said Filo.

"You're not getting the gist of what I'm saying unless you grow another thirty inches soon.

You won't be playing for the Lakers, the Clippers, or any other professional team," I said.

"I can always go to Japan and play," said Filo.

"One last student," said Ms. Berry

"Okay, Ralphie, what would you like to be?"

"No, teacher, that's not why I'm raising my hand."

"Teacher, I seen you on the bus yesterday."

"No, Ralphie, I saw you on the bus," I said.

"Oh, you seen me too?"

"No, I was correcting your English," I said.

"Did you or did you not see me on the bus?"

"No, I wasn't on the bus," I said.

"Then how come you said you seen me on the bus? The whole class heard you."

"Leave the bus alone!" I shouted. "I have a car, I don't ride buses. Now, what would you like to be when you grow up?"

"Oh, I don't know, maybe a bus driver," said Ralphie. The class laughs.

"Class, in two months, we are going to have Career Day. Please pay rapt attention to the speakers. Some of you may have to reassess your future goals," I said.

"Class, let's clean up."

As I was walking past Principal Daniels' office, I shouted, "Boy, does my head hurt."

The Next Day

"Class, you have so many more opportunities than my generation. We didn't have computers in school."

Rollo raises his hand. "Teacher, did you have telephones in those days?"

"Yes, the telephone was invented in the 1870s," I said.

"Were you alive then?" asked Rizzo.

"No, that was more than 140 years ago."

"Just asking," said Rizzo, "you never know."

"What kind of classes did you have in those days?" asked Rizzo.

"Well, we had the basic classes, reading, writing, math, science, geography, history, and penmanship," I said.

"What is penmanship?" asked Rizzo. "Is it a man on a ship with a pen?"

"No, penmanship is your handwriting," I said.

"Teacher, don't nobody write anymore? After you learn to write your name, there is no need to learn to write anything else when you can text," said Rizzo.

"Okay, moving on," I said, "We also had home economics and sewing."

"Teacher," said Alex, "why would anyone take up sewing and home economics that's why we have children in 3rd world countries? By the way, if they are in the 3rd world, where are the other two worlds?"

I put my head down on my desk and cover my face. I raise my head and say, "Does anyone have any aspirin?"

"No teacher," said Rizzo, "I told you this is a drug free school."

I slowly raise my head. "Ms. Berry," said Maria, "did you have any clubs or organizations?"

"Yes, we did. There was the Thespian Society."

"What on earth was that?" Rollo leans over, and starts to whisper in Rizzo's ear "A thespian is a male."

"Stop Rollo!" I shouted. "A thespian is an actor who specializes in Greek tragedies."

"Oh, okay. I thought it was—

"We know," I interrupted. "And then there was animal husbandry."

"Oh, that's gross," said Rizzo, "who'd want to be a husband to an animal."

"No! No! No! Animal husbandry is the raising and caring of animals."

Anymore Questions?

"Teacher, when are we going on a field trip?" asked Rizzo.

"I'm not sure," I replied. "Where would you like to go?"

"Anywhere," said Rizzo.

"I do know that there are a few trips available to the museum."

"Anywhere but the museum," said the class.

"That's like staying at school," says Rizzo.

"I mean like going to an amusement park."

"I don't think that they will sponsor a trip to an amusement park."

"Yeah they will," said Rizzo. "Two of my brothers went."

Missy leans over and says, "You mean there are two more of you at home?"

"No, there are six more of us at home, but that's another story. Teacher, my brothers positively went on a school sponsored trip to an amusement park. I believe it was on June fifteenth."

"Oh teacher," said Missy, "that was grad night! You mean you had two brothers graduating on the same night? Were they twins?"

"No, one was slow and the other one just caught up with him."

Missy looks up and says, "Please tell me you don't have any sisters?"

"Oh, I have one but she's an identical twin. You have to have two girls if they are identical twins."

"No, one is a boy and the other one is a girl, they can't be identical."

"Why not?" asked Rizzo, "because they don't have the same body parts!" screamed Missy.

"Wait until I go home and tell them," said Rizzo.

"I think they already know," mumbled Missy.

"Class, let's get back to the field trip."

"Teacher," said Richie, "some schools visit other countries."

"Yes Richie," I said, "but you do realize that despite the fact that it is a school sponsored trip, your parents still have to pay for it, so let's keep that in mind. We'll come back to this at a later date."

"Class, as you know, we will be studying history as well as current events. Please pay particular notice of what is going on in the world. What outstanding sporting event ended in Europe four summers ago?"

Missy raises her hand "Yes, Missy."

"I believe you are referring to the London Olympics Games."

"Very good," I said.

"Ms. Berry," Rizzo raises his hand.

"Yes Rizzo."

"Teacher let me tell you about the event that I like best. I like swimming."

"Who's that big dude that eats a lot and keeps winning?"

"I believe his name is Michael."

"When are the next games gonna be?"

"In about six months."

"You mean I have to wait six months before I go to London to beat this guy?"

"No," I said, "the games will be in Brazil."

"How come?"

"Well Rizzo, they rotate every four years."

"Now I have to go to Brazil to beat him."

"I didn't know that you could swim," I said.

"I can't," said Rizzo.

"Then how do you expect to beat the best swimmers in the world?"

"I watch my dog swim, so how hard can it be?"

"You may need a backup plan, but don't count on the 2016 Olympics."

"Teacher, do they have Olympics for pets?" asked Rizzo.

"No!" I shouted. "Is there any more business? If not, then clean up so we can go."

"Teacher, teacher," said Richie. "Can we have a pet? Like in kindergarten?"

"Oh, that's right. Clyde our pet hamster. Weren't you in charge of him?"

"Yes, and his death was ruled an accident. He accidentally committed suicide. In fact, I think it was called peticide. He leaped to his death, but wasn't he in a cage?" asked Brittany.

"I know," said Richie, "which made it all the more difficult to understand."

"Hey, teacher," said Richie, "*Wild Kingdom's* on tonight. Maybe we can find a pet there."

"Richie," I said. "It has to be domesticated and caged. I believe *Wild Kingdom* is about wild beast!"

"So what does that mean?" asked Richie.

"It means it can't be wild and it has to be low maintenance."

"Does it have to be alive because I can bring in some road kill?"

"Yeah, let's bring in a dead pet. It's less work for me. Besides, if it's dead, we would have to take it to a taxidermist."

"Teacher, what do taxes have to do with it?"

"Richie, I want to see your parents real soon."

Before We Leave

"Class, I have a couple of announcements to make. After school tomorrow there will be tryouts for the track team and on the following day, there will be tryouts for cheerleaders."

"I'm so glad the track tryouts are first, so that if I don't make the team, I can become a cheerleader," said Rizzo.

"Okay, what's your best event?" asked Rollo.

"I'm not sure that's why I'm entering all of them. Besides, anyone can run, jump, and skip.

I've been doing that since I was a little kid, and one of them should pay off." "Okay take your best shot. How about throwing that big black ball?" "You mean the shot put?" asked Rollo.

"You only weigh ninety-eight pounds and the ball weighs twenty pounds, you do the math. You couldn't make the baseball team because you couldn't throw the ball to first base. In fact, you couldn't even make the girl's team. Do you think they'll let me roll the ball?"

"No" screamed Rollo, "pick another event. Okay, how about that long spear?"

"You mean the javelin? No Dude, you'll accidently kill somebody."

"Wait a minute," said Rollo, "I heard that if you could run around the track twelve times then you would automatically make the cross-country team. You know you will need to eat and drink before you run around the track twelve times."

"We only have thirty minutes before the trials, where am I going to find any food?" asked Rizzo.

"Well, I'm not going to be able to go to the cafeteria but listen, you can. Go over to the cafeteria and look hungry, thirsty, and weak. Dude when you are forty pounds overweight that won't fly. But I have an idea. How much money do you have on you?"

"Oh, about $2.00 in change," said Rizzo.

"We have about thirty minutes before the trials, okay, let's go over to the afternoon kindergarten class and bribe them out of their snacks."

"Great."

Twenty minutes later. "How much food did you get?"

"I got twelve snack packs. I told you little kids can't count."

"Okay," said Rollo, "I'll stand at the edge of the track and every time you pass by, I'll hand you a snack."

"Good idea," said Rizzo.

"Hurry, we only have five minutes before the gun goes off."

"What gun?" said Rizzo, "Man this ain't no violent sport is it?

"Just go to the line," said Rollo, "and when you hear the gun, then run."

"What's all this talk about a gun? You'll bet I'll run if somebody has a gun. I thought guns were illegal at school. Runners take your places."

The gun goes off. "Rizzo" hollered Rollo, "slow down ain't nobody shooting at you. Rizzo slow down." All of a sudden the announcer states, "Runner down, call the paramedics."

"This is a disaster," said Rollo, "I hope he is in good enough shape to try out for cheerleader."

The Next Morning

"Class, before our books arrive this week, I have a few questions to ask so I'll have some idea as to where you are in geography."

"Where would you find Victoria Falls?" I see a hand in the back. "Yes Lenny," I said. "You mean Victoria Fell? I think somebody pushed her."

"Okay," I said as I shook my head. "Victoria Falls is on the continent of Africa. It borders Zimbabwe and Zambia on the Zambesi River. Approximately 24.8 billion gallons of water go over the falls every twenty-four hours."

"Man," said Lenny, "that's more than our fountain outside."

"Moving on" I said.

"Oh," I see a hand in the back, "Yes Rizzo."

"How do you know that, maybe it's moved?"

"I don't think so," I said as I hold my head in my hand.

"Teacher, didn't the news say that we are in a drought? Why can't they send us some water?"

"How would they get it here?" I asked.

"Maybe they can ship through the ocean." The class laughs.

"Class, you need to take school more seriously. Now get serious! Who attacked Pearl Harbor?

Yes, Richie."

"Not me, I don't even know the girl."

"Okay," I said, "you want to play it this way? For homework tonight write fifty facts about Victoria Falls and fifty facts about Pearl Harbor. I'm also giving you a map of the United States. You have two weeks to learn the states and their capitals. After you learn them we will move on to the rest of the world.

"Class dismissed!"

As I walked passed Mr. Daniels' office, I howled, "I now have a headache and I'm dizzy. I hope it's not a brain tumor."

Monday Morning

"Rollo," says Rizzo, "it's bad enough that we have to learn stuff in our own country, now we got to know where the rest of the world is. I don't understand why we have to learn this. My brother's girlfriend is from a country that didn't even exist a few years ago, and may be gone by the time we get out of school."

"Yes," said Rollo, "but the people in the United States have to know where these countries are."

"But why?" asked Rizzo.

"So we will know where to send the foreign aid money."

"Oh, makes sense to me now."

"Well, let's go to the library and look for maps."

"Okay," said Rizzo. Rizzo comes back with several maps.

"Where did you get these maps?" asked Rollo. "These are pre-Civil War maps."

"What does that mean?"

"It means they are too old for the test. They don't have Alaska, or Hawaii and some of the Western States."

"I thought Alaska was in Canada near the North Pole, and that Hawaii was near some water. I said, what does that have to do with our U.S. map test?"

"Are you sure you don't want my sister to study with you? She only charges 50¢ per hour."

"Does she take credit cards, because I have one?"

"I don't think so."

"Does she extend credit?"

"Nope," said Rollo. "But what I do know is that she is good at what she does and she makes a lot of money."

"What does she do with her money?"

"I'm not sure. I think she puts it into a 401K."

"What's that?" asked Rizzo.

"I don't know. It might be some kind of piggy bank because she says that she will be rich by the time she turns twenty-one."

The next day in class.

"Are you sure you don't want me to get my sister to study with you? I'll even pay for it," said Rollo.

"Why would I want you to do that?"

"Because you don't know Jack."

"Who's Jack?" asked Rizzo, "Is that the new dude?"

"No," said Rollo, "it's just an expression."

"An expression of what?" asked Rizzo.

"You know teacher, what I don't like about this class, first you make us go to the Bulls eye Store (you mean target, Missy mumbles) and then you make us get a dictionary so that we can know what you're talking about, and now I'm looking for some dude named Jack that don't exist. That ain't teaching."

"That isn't teaching" I said.

"So you agree with me," said Rizzo.

"No, I was just correcting your English," I said.

Test Day

"Rizzo."

"Yes teacher."

"Why do you have your maps out, and why are they pre-civil war maps?" I asked.

"Oh, I'm not taking the test," said Rizzo.

"What do you mean? You either take the test or you are going to detention," I said.

"Oh, I'm planning on going to detention that's why I bought this grocery bag full of food. I plan on being in detention for quite a while," he said smiling.

"Rizzo, would you and your bag of food meet me in the principal's office after school?" I asked.

"Okay teacher, you want a pop tart?" asked Rizzo.

"I want to see your parents or guardians immediately," I replied.

"They can't come because they always have headaches," said Rizzo.

The Next Day

"Class, we are going to have a School Fair. We are going to have booths, arts and crafts, and entertainment. Does anyone want to participate?" I asked.

"Yes," said Rizzo.

"What is the nature of your act?" I asked.

"I want to put on a ventriloquist act," said Rizzo.

"Great," said Missy, "now we will have two dummies on stage."

"Rizzo," I said, "you know that you will have to audition for the part." "Okay, let me go to my locker and get my dummy."

"You actually have a dummy in your locker?" asked Missy, "Why doesn't that surprise me?"

Rizzo then goes to his locker and gets his dummy. He then finds out that the audition is immediately after school and that Missy was one of the judges. After the audition, Missy goes up to Rizzo and says, "You're not supposed to move your lips, mouth, and jaws."

"I'll bet you can't do it without moving your lips," said Rizzo.

"I know," said Missy, "that's why I didn't try out for ventriloquism, and besides, I don't keep a dummy in my locker."

"All right! All right! May I sing a song?" asked Rizzo.

"Only if you promise to go straight home," said Missy.

After a few notes, Missy yells. "Please find me a buzzer! Rizzo, go home!"

"Next up," said Missy

Rizzo got up. "I thought we decided that you were going home," said Missy.

"Yeah, but the dummy didn't get his audition," said Rizzo.

"Security," shouts Missy.

"All right! All right, I'm going home."

The End of the Week

"Class, let's get back to the field trip."

"Teacher," said Richie, "some schools visit other countries."

"Yes, Richie," I said," but you do realize that despite the fact that it is a school-sponsored trip, your parents still have to pay for it, so let's keep that in mind."

"Yes, Rizzo,"

"Let's visit LA."

"We are already in LA." I now pull out another gray strand.

"Good, then we won't have far to go," said Rizzo.

"Class, let's revisit our trip discussion on another day."

"Before you all leave, I want to see everyone's parents in two weeks for parent's conference. I especially want to see your parents or guardian, Richie and Rizzo."

"Hey, Rizzo are your parents coming?"

"No, remember I told you that they are deceased."

"So does that mean they're not coming?" asked Richie.

"It means they're dead," said Rizzo.

"You mean they're dead and deceased, wow that's rough. I'm sorry to hear that," said Richie.

"Who takes care of you?"

"Oh, they left their credit cards behind," said Rizzo.

"But won't you run out of credit one day?" asked Richie.

"Yeah," said Rizzo, "but hopefully we will be grown by then, but if not, I don't think they will put a bunch of kids in jail for trying to survive."

"True, but they may put you in foster care," said Richie.

"Oh, wow, I never thought of that. I better go home and have a talk with my brothers," said Rizzo.

"How many siblings do you have?" asked Richie.

"Oh, I don't have any siblings. I only have brothers and sisters," said Rizzo.

"Go get a dictionary," said Richie.

As I'm walking past Mr. Daniels' office, I screamed. "I have a headache and it's getting worse each day!"

This time, I got a reply from Mr. Daniels. "Ms. Berry, please come in."

"Mr. Daniels, my head hurts. I'm dizzy and my hair is turning gray. In addition to that, I'm screaming and hollering at everyone I see. I'm even suffering from road rage. I almost ran over a squirrel!" I said.

"Yes, I know," said Mr. Daniels.

"I think they're trying to drive me crazy with their foolishness," I said.

"I know they are," replied Mr. Daniels, "and you know how? Well, it has to do with a conversation I overheard a couple of weeks ago," said Mr. Daniels.

"Well, what did they say?" I inquired.

"They said, 'let's drive the new teacher crazy!'" said Mr. Daniels.

"And you're just telling me now," I said.

"Ms. Berry, that's what they do best at their age. It's just a phase they're going through, they'll outgrow it," said Mr. Daniels.

"Ms. Berry, you have to realize that these children can't live up to our past expectations. Their lives are different from previous generations. Many more of these children are from single parent houses, with one parent trying to fulfill two roles. Some have been exposed to drugs and violence, even physical abuse. You have to lighten up on them. And Ms. Berry," said Mr. Daniels.

"Ms. Berry, I know that they were difficult, but embarrassing them, being sarcastic, really doesn't work. It's not the way to go. Because of their low self-esteem, they act the way they do, and we don't want to add to their problems.

"The other reason I called you in my office is to tell you I found a teacher for them. I know that you are probably relieved because you don't have to finish your thirty days. So you will be free to go this Friday, or you can stick around a little longer and try to fix the problem."

"I'll think it over. But I feel that I didn't accomplish anything."

"Ms. Berry, you accomplished more than you think. At least you showed up. The last teacher was absent more than she came, and when she did come, she kept her head down most of the day. And when she really got upset, she went into the closet, that's how she got locked in the closet."

The Next Morning

"Class, I'll be gone in a few days and I want to tell you, I've learned a lot from you."

"Ms. Berry," said Rollo, "we know nothing."

"You know a lot more than you think you do," I said. "You know who adults," I said.

"Now, class, let's forget the past and let's make this a fun week. Let's have a great party on Friday!"

Friday Morning

"I can't believe today may be my last day. I can't wait to see their faces as I give them each a gift."

As I opened the door, it was I who was surprised. There was a huge banner across the room and it read, *Teacher, Don't Go*!

I have a lot to think about. Maybe I should stay and try to fix this.

To be continued…

Printed by Libri Plureos GmbH in Hamburg, Germany